The Judas Ear

Also by Anna Journey

The Judas Ear

POEMS

ANNA JOURNEY

Louisiana State University Press
Baton Rouge

Published with the assistance of a subsidy from the
University of Southern California

Published by Louisiana State University Press
lsupress.org

LSU Press Paperback Original

Designer: Barbara Neely Bourgoyne
Typeface: Chaparral Pro

Cover photograph: Untitled, 2012, by Karen Jerzyk

Library of Congress Cataloging-in-Publication Data
Names: Journey, Anna, 1980– author.
Title: The Judas ear : poems / Anna Journey.
Description: Baton Rouge : Louisiana State University Press, [2022]
Identifiers: LCCN 2021030869 (print) | LCCN 2021030870 (ebook) | ISBN
    978-0-8071-7661-0 (paperback) | ISBN 978-0-8071-7742-6 (pdf) |
    ISBN 978-0-8071-7743-3 (epub)
Subjects: LCGFT: Poetry.
Classification: LCC PS3610.O6794 J83 2022 (print) | LCC PS3610.O6794
    (ebook) | DDC 811/.6—dc23
LC record available at https://lccn.loc.gov/2021030869
LC ebook record available at https://lccn.loc.gov/2021030870

for my parents: Cindy and Tim Journey

Contents

THREE

FOUR

My warm gratitude to the editors and staff of the following publications in which these poems first appeared: *Aethlon:* "Slaughterama"; *Blackbird:* "Experimental Perfume Class in Which I 'Scent' the Folkloric Witch Baba Yaga" and "My Grandparents' Velvet Painting of *The Last Supper*"; *The Georgia Review:* "The Copper Pillowcase," "Hans Christian Andersen Feared Being Buried Alive," and "My Dulcimer Teacher Joellen Works as a Psychotherapist"; *The Kenyon Review:* "The Judas Ear" and "Lullaby Interrupted by the Stump of the Mammoth Tree"; *The Los Angeles Review of Books:* "Bodylore"; *Narrative:* "Golden Egg" and "Invertible Head as a Basket of Fruit"; *The New Yorker:* "Unconditional Belief in Heat"; *Prairie Schooner:* "Dead Man's Lashes," "Elegy for Paul, Who Died without a Stomach," "In Texas Scents Traveled Faster," and "My Gun"; *The Southern Review:* "Altos de Chavón," "For the Actor Luke Perry, Who Chose to Be Buried in a Biodegradable Funeral Suit Infused with Mushroom Mycelia," "I Donate to the Fundraising Campaign for the NASA-Designed Fragrance Eau de Space," "Portrait of an Ex-lover as a Hillbilly Satyr," and "Remember the Meningitis Couch?"; *Verse Daily:* "For the Actor Luke Perry, Who Chose to Be Buried in a Biodegradable Funeral Suit Infused with Mushroom Mycelia" (reprint).

"Elegy for Paul, Who Died without a Stomach" is in memory of Paul Otremba.

My abiding thanks to the folks at LSU Press, especially James W. Long and Neal Novak. Gratitude to Jessica Faust and Sacha Idell, coeditors of *The Southern Review.* Thank you to Jacqueline Osherow.

Gratitude to Linda Gregerson, Terrance Hayes, and Maggie Millner.

I'd like to acknowledge the generous support of the University of Southern California, particularly the most recent sabbatical and research funds that gave me the time and resources to complete this book.

Thank you to Karen Jerzyk for allowing me to use her untitled photograph on the cover of this poetry collection.

Love and gratitude to David St. John.

Acknowledgments

one

The Judas Ear

I invited the apostle to my stir-fry
       dinner by accident. I shook
into my smoking wok a packet of dried

wood ear mushrooms—the ones I'd bought
       from a farmers' market. I threw in
a handful of broccoli, carrots, snap peas,
          halved Brussels. My husband

added the firm tofu he'd cubed
       on our walnut block. As the veggies

seared, David set the table while I stirred
       the crackling mélange right-handed
with a wooden spoon, held a cell phone
         in my left. I decided to look up

the mushroom's other common names
       and found one—the Judas ear—that made me
drop my spoon, sent hot canola
         spitting at my wrist. The mushroom

looks like a whorled and ridged
       human ear sprouted from a tree trunk,
its canal tipped down as if listening for gossip,
         a far-off cough. Its flesh:

henna-colored, peach, or taupe. And it grows—
       this is the biblical part—on decaying bark,
including the rotted logs

and stumps of elders: same species of tree
       from which the suicide Judas
hangs himself after he learns Jesus
         will be crucified. All I'd

bargained for were mushrooms, but as I stared
            into the wok, I watched the Judas ears unfurl,
their dried fibers now plumped and sweet
                in the bubbling teriyaki. I thought of Dalí

posed in a photograph, deadpan next to a huge
            replica of the human ear. I thought of Emily
Dickinson. In one of her poems, she imagines

all mushrooms as the cumulative
            Judas-face of nature, since fungi thrive
in death and rot, betray the carbon
                bonds that hold our bodies,
and our earth, together. She brands

the mushroom using Judas's surname:
            "an Iscariot." It was almost a dare:

the rehydrated mushrooms sitting there, the *Eat Me*
            hovering, like a prompt on Alice's
magical cakes in Wonderland. The last time

an Episcopal priest dropped a consecrated
            wafer on my eighteen-year-old tongue,

muttered, *The body of Christ, the cup
            of salvation,* I pressed the Host
to my wet palate until the bread crumbled.
                What would the communion of Judas

now make in my mouth? What was there to do
            except turn the gas burner off, grab
a serving spoon, give the wok

one final shake, wonder who would betray
            whom after the first bite.

Golden Egg

Name of the donation agency, which made me
the goose: twenty-two and waiting

tables at Bacchus on Meadow in grad school.
I had to inject myself with hormones each day

for a month to prod my ovaries. *Three grand a batch,*
I'd told my boyfriend, dropping the egg

donation forms in his lap. I'd ignored
his protests—*You've done way too much acid;*

your eggs are mutants—and filled out
the questionnaire. The only part of the agency's

paperwork that made me shiver was when I had
to pick The Photo for my donor profile:

the picture that showed me at my most blue-eyed
and strawberry blond, my zenith of pink-

cheeked and monetizing cuteness.
I knew which one. I had my mom mail it,

no explanation: me, three years old,
in overalls of lilac corduroy. I'm holding to my ear

a toy rotary phone's red plastic receiver
as I pretend to talk to my granny. One

chubby finger loops and loops through
the spiral cord. My huge grin: both rows

of baby teeth exposed. After donating eggs
one time, which paid—for six months—my rent,

I tried not to think about it: The Photo,
which, over years, has grown into Them. Children

I never wanted, I want you now
to know one thing: You can find me

in the rhymes of every rockabyed night
your real parents spent by your side,

soothing you. I'm not real to you,
not a whole body: a partial body, a scraping,

and what does that make me? Don't try
to find me by spit, by genetic

sleuthing, by *Are you my?* I hope you
have all of your fingers, your toes, that you

love the old stories, those about the dark
forests and the children who survived,

like Moses. I'm the golden goose who
dropped you into someone else's basket and flew.

Invertible Head as a Basket of Fruit

Natalia called her art project *Butt Garden:*
the cascading hump of pink roses
she crocheted and then attached to her ass,
like a nineteenth-century bustle. She waddled
across our apartment's living room,
modeling her creation. She'd made
Butt Garden for one of her classes in fashion
design at VCU, after spending the fall
semester in Paris, where she spoke fluent
French, English, Arabic. I was between
boyfriends that season, needed
a roommate for the spring

who didn't mind my late hours. *Laid back
art major preferred,* my flyer had said. I liked
her immediately: the way Natalia
referred to her boyfriend Dane
as "The Dane"; her taste for dolmas
packed in olive oil; how she could hold
at least ten glass-head pins in her mouth
at once while she worked on a dress
pattern. Natalia introduced me

to estate sales, where we'd shop for oddities
or fine china on Saturdays if we were both
home at the same time: floral-themed porcelain
for our windowsill set, a novelty hat
in the shape of a clam. Our favorite score:
an oversize poster-book of Renaissance artist
Giuseppe Arcimboldo's paintings—the strangest
of which are his invertible still lifes,
like the wicker basket of fruit that, when flipped
upside down, becomes a human head
wearing a gold crown, with apples for cheeks,

a pear for a nose, green grape bunches for hair,
and a row of red cherries for a lower lip. Flip
the image again and it morphs from portrait
back to still life. Natalia and I developed
a system: We each picked

a reversible Arcimboldo print, pinned it
to our bedroom door, and would turn
the poster to indicate our current mood:
human or *thing.* I chose *Invertible Head
as a Basket of Fruit* and Natalia tacked up
The Vegetable Gardener. Portrait meant
all-good but if we noticed still life
on the other's door, we knew to ask,
You okay, dude? One day I'd felt so-so
and had flipped my print from human face
to fruit basket, left the apartment to do
coke with Ed and Dan, didn't come back
until three in the morning. I found Natalia

still up, crying on the couch, knees tucked
under her chin. She'd worried
I was dead in some ditch—that I'd been too
sad to call—and had felt guilty she was
too late to stop me. After that, we decided to let
our prints remain witty Italian paintings
and not imbue their reversible positions
with personal significance. I remember
when I'd walked in the door, Natalia
had cried so hard the pins she'd held
between her lips had sunk straight through.

Post-retrieval

After the trigger-shot that stung
my hip, after the daily injections
of a hormonal stimulator,

after the final ultrasound
and the needle that sucked
my ova out, the egg donation

paperwork recommended Gatorade
and rare beef every day for a week
post-retrieval. *The bloodier*

the better, one nurse at the clinic
had said with a wink. I think
the hardest part afterward wasn't

the bloating or sharp cramps
or even my uncontrollable
weeping and shrieks at my boyfriend,

who'd warned me not to go
through with the procedure
just to earn three grand. I'd quit

my job waiting tables. *You don't*
understand, I said, waving
a forked bite of the flank steak

he'd broiled with soy sauce
and lime, the cut that left our
serving plate pooled in a watery

pink ooze flecked with red garlic.
I feel like I'm chewing on the meat
of the unborn, you know? He

didn't know. He nodded anyway,
though, rifled through our fridge
to find the sweetest barbecue sauce

we owned—the Kansas City
variety mixed with ketchup and dark
molasses. He dumped a heavy glug

over my steak to disguise its blood-
and-salt taste with sugar, making sure
to completely cover the rarest bites.

Remember the Meningitis Couch?

That petal pink three-seater from the Baptist
thrift shop on Broad Street? Its ribbed texture

had the channeled dust, striped the upholstery's
piping grey. You took eight months to tell me

your used couch came with a warning tag: that the sofa
had sat for decades in the waiting room of a Richmond

meningitis clinic. Although I haven't thought of that gnarly
pink couch in ages, or your apartment on Lombardy

where we started our seven years, I've been thinking
about contagion lately, here on the edge of April

in this viral spring. From my balcony I watch a blue
flap of lacecap hydrangea flatten

on the sidewalk. No, it's someone's dropped
nitrile glove. We snuggled all spring on that grizzled

pink couch before we ditched it
in the side alley. We didn't want to bring it with us

in the move. But before we trashed the sofa,
your friend the blues singer crashed

in the living room with a brunet psyche major
he'd met that night at his gig. As you and I lay in bed,

we heard a weird groan, and you flung open our door
on a blow job—the woman's face bobbing just above

Andrew's crotch and the couch's center butt cushion.
You slammed the door, whispered, *Oh, God! Oh, God!*

until I sat up to shush you: *Dude, it's just a blow job.* You flipped
the white sheet over your head, like a nun, finally

muttered your confession: You knew viral meningitis
died quickly on surfaces, that the sofa wouldn't infect us,

but the idea of *sex* on those once teeming cushions
freaked you out. You stopped explaining as I collapsed

backward on the bed, as I rolled
from side to side, laughing. Right now, I could use

a laugh like that. That's why I keep thinking
of that old sofa during this spring of the body

count, how we sprawled all season on a used
couch that could've killed us had it sat for less

time in the Baptist thrift shop. Even though
we no longer know each other, I like to remember

how we crept into the side alley, at midnight,
beers in hand, to stand in front of the pink

sofa we'd dragged between garbage cans
and fringed wisteria. I like to remember

that last glance you shot me before
we stepped up, each hurled a lit match.

Flatback

Could be a bran pancake
or a vanilla-sex position

yet it's the condition
that prompts people

to compliment my posture:
Did you take ballet?

Play the cello?
Flatback syndrome:

It's what my doctor calls
"an abnormally straight spine,"

which you'd think would be fine
except for the fibrous knots

hard as peach stones
seeding my thoracic back

as if gravel had nerves,
as if the gods cursed me

with perfect posture.
In the fairy tale, the Sea Witch

gives the Little Mermaid
a perfect human body, and,

in Hans Christian Andersen's
version, each step she takes

with her new legs feels
like walking on knives. What

former creature was I
before the ache, down

in the water where my body
once moved, weightless,

the whole ocean
holding me up.

Bodylore

Once there was a myth
for this: an ache,
a loss, a fairy

who carried it off.
Tooth Fairy,
I'm talking to you.

I've got a hurt
I don't know what to do
with, a stuck one,

a stubborn, gnarled
place in which the self
sits like

an interlocutor
in all this knotted meat.
If I could, I'd unbraid

that wall hanging
of driftwood and coarse
rope woven

with gristle and teeth
that other people see
as *Anna's back* but is actually

a demon macramé.
Come back, Tooth Fairy.
You took what I was

too young to give
with real understanding
and without so much

as a wiggle or yank. Come
stand here and
cut this out of me.

I Donate to the Fundraising Campaign for the NASA-Designed Fragrance Eau de Space

I'm over my vanilla nose, over
the early nineties cologne that's simmered

on my neck and wrists
since eighth grade: Vanilla Fields. I've worn the scent
so long I don't even notice

its warm sugar on my skin: that mix
of vanilla bean, mimosa, and jasmine. Decades ago,

NASA developed Eau de Space
to help astronauts adjust
to the smell of the cosmos. The fragrance?

Seared steak, raspberries, gunpowder, and rum.

One former astronaut describes the smell
of outer space as brimstone,

as if a witch had just passed through, only to ruin
the simile by explaining it: The aroma's

probably just the vacuum sucking
trace chemicals from the walls of the craft.
In past years

I considered acquainting myself
with the void, decided

not to. I've chosen, now,
to donate to NASA's campaign
for the fragrance—the funds raised will help make

Eau de Space widely available. This is the kind of
campaign I like. If I ever get my hands

on a vial, I'll spritz both wrists,
flip off the overhead light,
sit in the dark for a minute

and sniff. Once I adjust to the scent—
seared steak, raspberries, gunpowder,

and rum—I hope my nose will grow
numb to it: the void that once called me,

yawing, infinite, now
soft and tame as faded vanilla,
thin as a wrist.

Cat-Cow

I can shift species, depending on my breath's
rhythm and my spine's

shape: arch, sag,

arch, sag, from feline
to bovine
and back. In the yoga pose Cat-Cow

I'm supposed to be increasing
my spine's flexibility:
hands and knees

on the mat in Tabletop's neutral position,
then rounding my vertebrae into a feline arch
so I become
every cat

I've ever loved: Banjo, Deetjen,
The Bean, Charlie, Willow, Pye.

I'd call Jellybean, my first cat in adulthood,

Walnut Brain ever since I'd read the anatomical
comparison in a science article
and felt I had, momentarily,

gained X-ray vision. And when
Bean's kidneys

broke at thirteen and she died—after
an ER vet injected her in my arms as we sat

in front of a wallpaper-sunset, lilac streaks over a lake—
I couldn't stop replaying the sound
of her suffering: a low, rolling cry

like she'd always been wild
instead of that chest-sitting sphinx and mischievous

calf-nipper. For weeks I howled
with grief so wild I couldn't breathe.
It took a long time to breathe

like this: arch, sag, arch, sag into bovine
and back to cat.
When I'm All Cow

for the moment, I barely know
my own face in the mirrored sliding doors

of my bedroom closet: my slow,
dopey eyes, cud-dumb mouth. For the moment
I am every bite

of beef I've ever eaten—ground,
sirloin, porterhouse, ribeye, T-bone, flank.

For a second I notice an expression in my eye
so frank I almost mistake it
for bravery: a face so calm

it says I'd step
right into the chute

that leads to the bolt-gun. This is my meditation,

why my spine can't stay neutral
for long. I move in the polarized

arc of the minute and the minute

betrays us with its tricks
and mnemonics: Cat-Cow, arch, sag, arch,
Marjaryasana,
Bitilasana, bone

and breath. This moment:
hold it
until it's over

and you decide which animal.

two

Experimental Perfume Class in Which
I "Scent" the Folkloric Witch Baba Yaga

for Saskia Wilson-Brown, at the Institute of Art and Olfaction

I sniff the drop of beaver animalic
called castoreum on my blotter strip—

the musk my perfume teacher Saskia describes
as "old people smell" and makes me

think of vanilla ice cream threatened
by a nearby mothball. I'm trying to find

the right mix of scents for Baba Yaga,
the Slavic witch. In folktales she lives

in a woodland hut that walks on chicken feet
and she eats Russian children,

but only the bad ones. In most
versions of the story, she helps a little girl—

who'd gotten lost searching for turnips—return
to her family. Last week, my mom and dad

put a for-sale sign on my childhood house
and I wished for some magic

to stop it. Remodelers wrecked our kitchen's
Spanish tile with granite, knocked out

a wall. Instead of riding an airborne broom,
Baba Yaga flies in a giant spice mortar that she rows

with an oarlike pestle. For the witch's
iron teeth, Saskia suggests I try a drop of rose oxide

for the way the compound conjures
both flower petals and a whiff of metal—breath

that blooms iron and rose. I like those
middle floral notes but need an earthier base

to soften and anchor the raw fragrance, so Saskia
hands me an anonymous blotter strip. I sniff,

nearly gag on the rotten scent she tells me is civet:
extract from the anal glands of a Malayan wildcat

whose aroma evokes the smell of decaying bodies
or fecal matter yet when diluted for perfume adds

"warmth" and "shimmer" to a scent. *Doesn't have
to be pretty,* Saskia says. *We're telling a story.*

But I already love the tale: I can finally inhale
my favorite childhood witch

in the third dimension—olfaction wafting her
right off the page in her personal

animal bouquet. The fragrance I name
"Baba Yaga's Kiss" and dribble from a pipette's

glass stem onto my wrists will later derange
my two Siamese cats, who won't stop

licking my skin. Before class ends, Saskia
shows me an alternative method to sniffing

coffee beans to "reset" a scent-swamped nose:
Smell your armpits—you are your own white noise.

With the rot of undiluted civet still hanging
in my nostrils, I think: *No one alive*

could smell like this. So I jam my nose
into my right pit for a sniff, flush out the dead

witch, return to my own body for a minute
and remix her. I stir my perfume until the civet

warms as it spreads—base note that will make
all of Baba Yaga shimmer.

Unconditional Belief in Heat

I would've stabbed the man's hand
        had he not jerked it away—this is what I usually say
toward the end of the story. The man

had pried back the right vinyl side panel
        of my living-room window's A.C. unit, ripped
the accordion-style flap from its mounting track,
        and began palming the wall inside
my first-floor apartment. My ex

had left at the beginning of summer and Natalia
        wouldn't move in until spring, so I lived alone
that June in Richmond, in the back bottom suite
        of a shoebox-shaped fourplex
set perpendicular to the street. In the story

I've told for almost twenty years,
        I'm a junior in college toweling my wet hair
as I walk from my bathroom through the hall,
        headed to my bedroom, at two in the morning.
I notice a flicker of motion from the living-

room window: a human hand
        flopping, like live tilapia, through
the side panel's bent vinyl, the limb shoved in
        up to the elbow. I charge at the arm, yell,

I see you, motherfucker, and the hand
        jerks back. The man flees. When I call 911
and reach, incredibly, a busy signal, I phone Ed instead,
        who will drive over, remove his old A.C. unit, take it
to his new place. Until Ed arrives, I hover
        near the pried-back vinyl

gripping a butcher knife. I would've stabbed
        the hand that tried to steal my A.C. This is how
I tell it: I once thwarted a thief and he's lucky
        I let him keep all his fingers. Last night,

on the phone with my best friend, I retold
        the story and Alicia paused, then said,
He wasn't after your A.C. Twenty years ago,
        she must've said the exact same thing to me,
but I'd brushed it off, positive

I'd terrified a thief. It was June in Richmond
        and I was young and held an unconditional belief
in a heat made utterly obscene
        from humidity. It got so hot I could imagine
someone getting high and thinking, *Goddamn,*
        I need some A.C. My living-room window faced

a small side lawn that abutted the back garden
        of a rich person's town house: a low wall
of calico brick from the nineteenth century
        with an overhanging fringe of dogwoods that had
by that point in summer expanded into a fat

green canopy. At two in the morning
        no one would've seen him climb in—quick
flicker between the brick and my window.
        I know years ago Alicia said the same thing,

but I had to stop believing in my own
        permanence to hear her. But I still
believe in—deep summer, Virginia—
        that heat.

Altos de Chavón

I had to quit waiting
tables at Bacchus, in Richmond, that summer
because of the hot-and-cold switch. Each time

I reached for a guest's ice water to refill it,
the pint glass burned my fingertips as if
I traced the copper sides
of a boiling teakettle. And each time I ladled

lobster bisque from the soup warmer
into white melamine bowls,
carried the appetizers to a table, my palms
felt as if they packed the frozen
sides of a snowball. I had to quit
that job. I had to quit giving

blow jobs, too, since my boyfriend's dick
had turned to an icicle in my mouth—
his cocksicle, we called it. Patrick had the same

neurological derangement: If he reached
beneath my arms for a hug, my pits
chilled him like arctic caves. His steaming coffee
tasted iced, he said, so he added *real* cubes
from our freezer to fool
his tongue. We'd gotten ciguatera,

a rare type of fish poisoning,
in the Dominican Republic, while visiting
La Romana with his father. We stayed
in the small sailboat his dad co-owned
with another orthodontist and kept docked
in Casa de Campo's marina. The boat

bobbed among the uber-rich's white yachts,
the resort's scrappiest derelict. Privately, I sneered at it
to Patrick as we unpacked our bags
in the V-shaped sleeping space in the forepeak
and I saw our accommodations: twin wooden berths
hard as park benches covered
with inch-thick foam. *Some vacation,*

I muttered. The first night, when we dined
with his dad—the three of us at a table
on the waterfront deck—I glanced down
from the teal waves and white sand to scan
the menu, recalled my biologist father's warning:
Don't eat the reef fish. He'd told me
that certain fish feed along coral reefs
in the Caribbean and ingest

marine plankton that contain
a dangerous neurotoxin. Ciguatera
torments you far worse than regular food poisoning—
cramps, nausea, vomiting, but also
chills, muscle aches, fatigue, numbness
in the limbs, and the weirdest symptom
of all: the reversal

of hot and cold sensations. The tactile scramble
can drag on for months. I asked
the restaurant-server if grouper
was "a reef fish," and the man shook his head,
grabbed my menu. Patrick ordered
the grouper, too. Later, wracked with cramps,

we learned the intimate dimensions
of a small sailboat. All night

we staggered to and from the craft's
only head. *Grouper pooper,* we groaned,
moaning on the stiff boards that were our beds
for the next week. We hadn't realized

how long the symptoms would linger. That last evening,
still weak from fatigue, Patrick and I drove
alone to Altos de Chavón—an all-stone
faux-Spanish-colonial
replica of a Renaissance village

built on a riverside cliff. We wandered its
Mediterranean-style plazas: the narrow
cobblestone streets, the arched porticos,
the cigar shops, the terracotta-roofed
pottery studios, the stone fountains. We stopped
to sip guava juice on a café's cliff-edge
veranda, then touched the rough walls
of St. Stanislaus pocked with coral,
ash-white, and taupe. The neurotoxin

had initially numbed our hands enough
so we could lace fingers without freezing the tips—
the full-on sensory switch would come. At dusk,
most other tourists left or ducked inside
one of the restaurants, but we remained
in the emptying plaza as lanterns began to glow.
We hoped to see the famed colony

of feral cats crawl from the royal palms
and swarm the limestone. We'd heard the animals
overran the village at night, searching
for scraps. A shaggy troupe

of around twenty calicos soon emerged
from behind a tiered fountain to circle us,
mewling. More leaped down from a red mahogany's
lowest branch. *I feel like the Pied Piper,* I said,
but with cats. We called them to us, led the animals—
their claws clicking over cobbles—into the mock-
Grecian amphitheater, then up its panoramic
stone steps until, at the top, panting, we could see
the Chavón River ripple with lights. I only half-noticed,

as I stroked a cat's back and it arched under my palm,
the fur's unusually needled sensation, a sort of electric
neural hum. I thought: *Just grimy,* not
My body is wrong.

Before we flew back to Virginia, Patrick snapped
a photograph of me standing in the shade, grinning
as my hand cups a dangling mango. It's impossible
to tell from my face that I can't really *feel*
the fruit's cool rind, just a warm
neuropathic ache. It would take

two weeks before I could sense *anything's* skin,
three months before I stopped perceiving
each nudge or brush to the extreme,
and wrong. That long summer, ice water
shocked my hands like a fried socket
and a man's flesh froze at my touch.

The Copper Pillowcase

I once dated a man so vain he slept
exclusively on a pillowcase made of copper

oxide fibers. Dan's special anti-aging
pillowcase, he'd explained as we lay nose

to nose in his bed, improved blood
circulation and acted as an anti-inflammatory—

the copper threads are supposed to smooth
fine lines, reduce wrinkles, promote collagen

growth. I nodded, said I could totally tell as Dan
reached to switch off the light. After that night

I never called him again. Ten years later
I ran into Dan as he sat in front of a short stack

of blueberry pancakes at a café in Richmond. At first
I saw him from the left side, only in profile,

and he looked as smooth and baby-faced
as he'd been when we were both twenty. I hoped

he wouldn't notice my eye's budding
gesture of a crow's-foot. Yet as he turned, began

to wave, I realized the whole right side of his face
drooped and sagged: the corner of his mouth,

his upper eyelid, his cheek's fat pad. I could barely
speak, remembering how he'd always slept

on his left side. The copper pillowcase must've
perfectly preserved that half of Dan's face

as the rest of him creased and caved. Throughout
our small talk, my gaze moved from his dilated

pupils to his pancakes' blueberries, which had softened
and spread to a purple mush in the buttermilk.

We didn't have much to say except to list
the places we'd lived since we'd last

seen each other: his bouncing from Richmond
to Newport News and back, my stint in Houston

before I'd landed in Los Angeles. After we said
our goodbyes, I ran into a mutual friend

who told me about Dan's stroke, the one he'd had
at twenty-eight—maybe from doing

too much coke—which left one side of his face
paralyzed. I'd just finished reading a biography

of Hans Christian Andersen on the plane ride
to Virginia, so perhaps I'd been primed

to believe a copper pillowcase could erase
all traces of time on one half of a man's face,

dividing him into a lopsided hybrid
as a grotesque punishment for his vanity.

But Dan was just a thirty-year-old burnout
buttering a stack of purpled pancakes, and I

didn't know what to say as a drop of saliva
formed in the corner of his sagging mouth

and so absentmindedly touched the crease
of my own nascent crow's-foot, afraid

it might finally break across my right
temple with the full reach of its claws.

Slaughterama

Because Ed's armband tattoo was fresh and bled
its geometric repeating waves beneath the clear bandage
of Saran Wrap on his bicep, only I'd compete
in the annual bike event called Slaughterama
that year. Each spring, in Richmond, Virginia, hundreds
of crust-punks, sculptors, musicians, bike messengers,
baristas, grad students, tattoo artists, and other
heavily pierced locals toting six-packs of Pabst
descend on Belle Isle to watch the games. To get
to the island from the city's north bank, you have to cross
a suspension footbridge slung by steel cables
that sway over the muddy James. The games
are part carnival, part demolition derby
held in the tin-roofed ruin of Old Dominion
Iron and Nail Works—an open-air factory-shed
that resembles a rectangular horse arena. That spring's
competitions: tall-bike jousts, bike-chariot races,
conceptual tricycles, and unicycle boxing
with raw chicken tied to participants' hands
like gloves. And there's always some

shirtless bartender named Marty with a pentagram
squirted in Heinz 57 on his beer belly: one way
he helps his friends find him in the crowd. Ed,
my first college boyfriend, was a pot dealer
and glassblower of blobs so lumped and solid
he sold most of his art objects as "paperweights." He'd
introduced me to Slaughterama on one of our first dates.
Ed of the eye-twitch and white-boy dreadlocks that reached
his lowest vertebrae. Earlier that May, he'd helped me weld
two bike frames together to make a double-decker ride
so I could compete in the tall-bike jousting event
in which mounted participants lunge toward each other
grasping the extended ends of toilet plungers

like medieval lances. Since Belle Isle once housed
thousands of starved and lice-bitten Union soldiers
in the island's Civil War prison camp—whose grit

and silica now swirl through bicycle spokes—some
Slaughteramans wear thrift-store navy blazers in homage
to the dead's blue uniforms as a way to give
the finger to the Confederacy. The unofficial mantra
of the games: *Cheating is encouraged,* which means
people try to shove you off your bike or pelt your arms
and back with empty Pabst Blue Ribbon cans. *Even losers win—*

the games' other mantra, which I learned
firsthand when I didn't last a full minute
jousting a wiry woman with a half-shaved black bob
who shoved her toilet plunger hard into my right boob
and I toppled from my giant bike to the dirt.
People raced over, cheered, and poured their beers
on my forehead's crown and into my open
mouth, grabbed my wrists to raise my arms
into a victory "V." Ed pulled me up, his Saran-
Wrapped tattoo leaking a waterier ooze
as he kept drinking. I shook from adrenaline,
my left shin stripped of skin along four inches
of bone. But getting bloody with hundreds
of others was part of the fun

and also part of the dark edge that crept in at dusk
as the games ended. I could tell time by the state
of Marty's ketchup pentagram, which smeared and shed
its dried lines, changed shape over his stomach
like a sundial's moving shadow. The wounded bikers
would limp in a hooting troop back over the footbridge,
leaving Belle Isle's paths spattered, the leaves
of sweet gum and sassafras smudged as they

must've been some nights in that other century.
Sometimes a lucky biker would leave with the misshapen
lead mushroom of an antique bullet she'd picked
up and tucked in her pocket. I always hoped

to find one. That night I bandaged my shin while Ed
replaced the crusted Saran Wrap over his tattoo
with new layers, slept with that same arm
draped over my nude waist. His wound oozed for hours,
leaked a beer-thinned streak into my belly button.
When I woke I found in my innie a dried
red plug the shape of a thumb.

New Skin

For weeks I couldn't keep band-aids
from sliding off my hands. When I was a potter

in college and needed to cover a nick
on my fingers, regular bandages

got soggy from wet clay and sloughed
into the center of my pots. They swirled

at the bottom of the cylinder like a clock
gone wild. If one band-aid managed

to cling for an hour on my gashed pointer
or thumb, its edges would drag

a rough frieze into the stoneware
as I pulled the clay walls up from the spinning

wheel-head. I soon learned the secret
of throwing pots despite finger-wounds

from my ceramics teacher Steve: red-bearded
Chicago hippie in his mid-thirties who wore

thrift-store shirts (ironic Hawaiian, neon green,
pastel pink) and had a blunt but cheerful affect:

Get to work! If he saw me walking down
Hanover—street on which

we both lived—as I schlepped my massive
canvas portfolio to an eight a.m. drawing class,

he'd call out, *Good morning, Sunshine,*
as he pedaled past on his bicycle. He'd toss

in a wave, too, a quick sideways glance,
knowing how much I loathed

getting up early. Steve shared his on-campus
studio with his sweet Midwestern wife Kathy

who was also his artistic collaborator. They'd make
pots together: square sushi plates

brushed in black-and-white slips, Shino-glazed
coffee mugs with iron oxide linework,

triangular teapots with hollow
pillow-lids into which they sealed

little nodes of rolled clay so that, after firing,
you could lift the bisqueware lids

and rattle them like tiny maracas. I drank my
morning coffee from one of their mugs,

hoped it was Steve's thumb that raised
the whorled spiral on the inside. I liked to linger

in the doorway of his and Kathy's studio
wearing my black smock covered with my own

smeared handprints. They both listened to me
gripe about my live-in boyfriend Ed—

drug dealer and aspirational
glassblower-slash-painter I couldn't figure out

how to break up with. Steve delivered his advice
loudly, yet with affection—*What are you doing?*

Leave that guy already!—while Kathy offered
soft eye-contact, nods, salted

pretzels from a big sack. I couldn't stop imagining
Kathy dying—always painlessly

and in her sleep, never in a car wreck, never
from heart attack or stroke—so I could

comfort Steve in his grief, marry him and keep
Kathy's framed portrait on our mantle

as a memorial between the new
coffee mugs we'd make together:

Steve throwing the pots' clay bodies, me
attaching each pulled handle. I'd pat

his black lab—now *our* black lab—named
after a chemical compound used in clay-

mixing: Gerstley. During one of the first
weeks he was my art teacher, Steve heard me

cuss at a sodden band-aid dangling
from my wet knuckle and brought me

his bottle of antiseptic acetone called New-Skin,
which, when brushed on a wound,

left a flexible waterproof seal, like a swath
of clear nail polish. He had me rinse

my slurried hands and, holding my cut one
in his own, dabbed the liquid band-aid

along the open sliver, which stung
as the medicine dried. I almost

flirted, almost joked, *What would Kathy
think,* but instead I held the edge

of the industrial sink and asked if I could
copy that Grateful Dead show he had

blasting, right then, on the stereo. He blew
twice on my wound—*There you go*—then turned

to leave. I hoped that seal would hold,
and keep holding, as long as I needed it to.

My Gun

Looks like a power drill,
space-alien ray gun—black
with a neon-blue circle on the grip
panel. Triangular handle. It's useless
for bank-robbing, for muggings, for crimes
of passion, unless you count
my spine's abnormality
as a crime. I use my gun
on myself—percussive

massage gun that pummels
the paraspinal muscles with rapid
punches of its polyurethane fist. My favorite
of the gun's multiple attachments: the one
called "the cone," for its stabby
shape and the way it sticks
deep into scar tissue, breaks up
the old damage, or at least softens
the edges of the hardest
lumps. Once,

in Richmond, I lived across
the street from Lombardy Market,
where I'd buy six-packs of Harpoon
for the ale's malted-caramel taste
but mainly for its label's
trippy filigree of orange lotuses.
And buttermilk biscuits with pork sausage,
too, from the Southside biker dude
named Lucky who worked
the counter, and whose
black ponytail swung
with his movements. His beefy arms
and snake tattoo could seem

scary, except once he spoke
you realized he was sweet,
that he meant it when he called you
Honey. I'd sell him pot sometimes
during his breaks when he'd dart
out to my place, or rather
my boyfriend Patrick's place
in which I stayed along with his
childhood friend John, a recent
Iraq War vet. Because John woke up
most nights kickboxing the dark
as he hopped on his bed,
shouting as the steel springs
clanked like a muffled accordion,
Patrick finally had to put a padlock
on the inside of our bedroom door
and a second one on our side
of the shared bathroom.

During one of our fights, I slammed
the front door, shouted,
John needs to move! and, sobbing,
ran barefoot onto the sidewalk. I noticed
the glow of Lucky's cigarette cherry
flare across the street as he leaned
against the brick front
of the market. He didn't say anything
then, just pulled out another
cigarette, wiggled its white paper
tip the air, motioned me over. We smoked,
side by side, until I cleared my throat,
told him I was going to take a walk.
He said, *Wait,* ducked inside,
and came back with a single

paper-bagged Harpoon, handed it to me.
I lived on that block half a year
before I finally learned
the origin of Lucky's nickname:

that during an armed robbery at the market,
he'd emptied the register while held
at gunpoint, then raised his hands.
The robber aimed a pistol at Lucky's
forehead, point-blank, and pulled
the trigger. The gun jammed. After that,
Lucky made sure the neighborhood
knew he kept a loaded Colt
somewhere up front. Sometimes,

when I'm drilling my back
with my gun, I think of how Lucky
once stared down the barrel
of a real one. Even after I knew
the story I could never say more
to him than: *Want to swing by later?*
I just got more weed. Or:
Two biscuits today, sir. I'm massively
hungover. I never said

goodbye to Lucky when I moved
to Houston. Almost fifteen years
later, I've driven by Lombardy Market
many times on my visits
to Richmond, but I can't bare
to go inside. I'm afraid
Lucky won't be there. I'm worried
some stranger's face will
displace his if I look, so I just glance
once at the whitewashed brick,

avoid the upper half of the window.
If I balance the angle of my gun's
cone attachment so it points
straight down, let gravity drive in
the tip, the edges of the hard
scar tissue begin to break.

In Texas Scents Traveled Faster

because of the humidity
and heat. There, where the air
molecules and I were both

more volatile. Often,
after my boyfriend and I argued,
I slipped out

to the front porch's steps,
where it took less than a second
for the smell of our neighbor's

potted chives and Thai basil
to hit my nose, her blue
Tuscan rosemary. I knew

the names of her herbs
by those oak-finished garden markers
she'd posted, each one labeled

in white-painted cursive. I know
the name of my mother's
lost baby: Rosemary. That first-

trimester girl would've been
between my younger sister and me,
probably another red-haired

shit-talker. When I moved
from Houston to Los Angeles and into
another man's house, I didn't

notice his back patio's
rosemary for weeks, the plant
tucked in the shade of a rough

braid of hundred-year-old wisteria.
The shrub's aroma, in the dry
climate, didn't stretch

more than a foot from the edge
of the green needles. Their scent
sneaked up on me

only when I accidentally
drew close. Rosemary,
how will you meet me

when I die? Suddenly,
as in the humid
reek of a Texas side garden?

Or discreetly, at my elbow, in the slow
radius of a dry heat? I only
shake that namesake

herb over food when I have to,
when I make a certain
roasted potato recipe. So, surprise me,

Rosemary. Come quickly
or slowly when I die. I don't
want to know which way

it'll be. *Rōsmarīnum,* the Greeks
called it, meaning *dew*
from the sea. When I crumble

the flecked shrub over golden
fingerlings sliced and spread
along my sheet pan, its evergreen

scent resins my thumb tips: whiff
of crushed pine and camphor,
almost-sister, Rosemary.

My Childhood Neighbor Joey,
Who Kept a "Pet Fart" in a Pickle Jar

He must've craved a way to give
his nothing a scent, that ugly-
self stuffed in an empty
pickle jar, shut in,

like lightning bugs. Like the ones
my younger sister and I used to catch
with Joey, then release
into the two cedars that grew

between our houses, making
the fragrant red bark blink off
and on with neon. We'd play
in the cul-de-sac each night,

running from swing set to creek
to stilt-house with its pull-up
rope ladder. We'd stay out
until we could only half-see

our hands and our moms called us
in to dinner. Sometimes I wonder
what would've happened had Joey
opened his jar and released

that sealed-in stink he called
his "pet fart." Instead, he raised
the glass with both hands to shake
in my sister's face as a threat,

making her squeal. When Joey's
mom told my mom where
she'd found him—hanged
from a beam in his bedroom

closet—I knew I had to find
that jar and smash it. He was
so goofy that last week
no one noticed the brooding.

He was eleven. Me: ten.
I didn't know where he'd hidden
his bad joke—the last one
he'd ever make. I just needed

to take from his house what he
couldn't see, what I couldn't see.
I had to find that reek and let
the rest of the body out.

My Grandparents' Velvet Painting of
The Last Supper

I wasn't allowed to touch Jesus, Peter, or John,
or any apostle at all, their forbidden skins

fuzzed in peach acrylic over the black velvet's
short pile. My grandmother bought the kitsch

painting at a church fundraiser in Greenwood,
had my papaw hang it on their dining-

room wall. If she noticed my elbow
propped on the dinner table during our summer

visits to Mississippi, she'd point to Judas—
the only guest in *The Last Supper*

with his elbow plopped on the tabletop—
click her tongue. As a kid, sometimes I'd walk

past the velvet painting and try to brush
its plush surface with my shoulder "by accident."

But I'd chicken out since the apostles'
shocked expressions at Christ's news

about the future betrayal seemed aimed
at me, too. Judas's jaw, in the genre's

iconography, always sits lower
than the others' heads as a symbol

of his lowdown dirty nature and sinful
death by suicide. I'd learned what his skin

must've felt like much later, when I picked
out a pair of crushed velvet bellbottoms

at the mall in the mid-nineties. The color:
midnight blue. So if I ever needed

a little drama to keep me awake in Algebra II,
all I needed to do was rub the top of my own

velvet thigh to feel the body of Judas move
under my desk, his leg soft—a breathless

shade of blue. I never told my grandmother
her scolding at the supper table had just made

Judas seem more human than the other apostles:
crude-mannered, relatable, remembered

only for his greatest mistake. I like to recall
the smaller one: his elbow on the table, his hand

posed to lift a napkin to those twitching lips
as if the story he had to tell could wait.

three

Lullaby Interrupted by the Stump
of the Mammoth Tree

This is as close as I can get
to a lullaby. It's July—four months
into the virus, and sleeping

through the early morning exists
only as a memory, a relic
of the Before. Before I swirled

a silicone plug in my up-facing ear
to block out my husband's
breaths. Before every doorbell

knell became a threat. Before
I needed John Muir beside me
to ease my insomnia—his 1901

essay on the Big Tree, the sequoia,
recorded by a voiceover actor
for my favorite meditation app

as a "sleep story." On the audio
track, a woman reads Muir's ecstatic
descriptions of redwoods

in a soothing cadence, with a New Age
loop of birdsong, creek-burble,
and soft piano lullabyed

in the background. I like the way
the naturalist names the giant sequoia
the auld lang syne of trees and *nature's*

forest masterpiece, how he praises
its *thoroughbred look.* On our visit
to Muir Woods outside

San Francisco, my husband and I
once stood in front of a historical
display at the forest's entrance. We stared

at an old lithograph of the stump
of the Mammoth Tree—the twelve-
hundred-year-old sequoia felled

in the Sierra Nevadas by gold-rush
speculators in 1853. Loggers
had smoothed the colossal stump

for use as a dance floor for tourists
and their tea parties. The act of desecration
so enraged Muir that he wrote

the manifesto "The Vandals
Then Danced Upon the Stump!"
Something happens each time

I cue up the meditation track,
even though it's not Muir's
Scottish accent flickered in my ear

but the bedtime voice of a woman
named Christine who means
to lull me to sleep. I can't sleep

if I start to think of the fate
of the Mammoth Tree, of Manifest
Destiny, of that lithograph

Showing, according to the caption,
a Cotillion Party of Thirty-two Persons
Dancing on the Stump at one time.

I turned to my husband, said,
"It's like watching people dance
on a grave," as we turned to walk

through Bohemian Grove's
old-growth redwoods, the main trail
fringed in maidenhair ferns and fat

Jurassic horsetails. This was back
in the Before. Before we began
rushing off paths in Topanga

to dodge other hikers coming
up the canyon. Before we cinched
bandanas around our necks to yank

over noses and mouths. Before
I needed John Muir as much
as the redwoods needed his words

that are more than a "sleep story,"
more like an elegy for the beginning
of the end of our world,

which waits like the planed stump
of a sequoia on which vandals, dressed
for a tea party, keep up their dance.

Radial Thoughts on the Surface Tension of Holes

He'd deliberately cracked the clay bong his student
had made, my college ceramics teacher Steve once told me.

He'd unloaded the bisqueware from the gas kiln named Hamada
and smacked the vessel's lip against a shelf, chipped

the mouthpiece so no one could smoke from it. Even though
we weren't allowed to make ashtrays, shot glasses, or bongs

in Steve's wheel throwing class, Jen had disguised
her banned project by calling it a "bud vase." She'd claimed

the small hole cut in her pot's flared belly—clearly designed
for a pull-out slide—was meant for the green stem of a single

rose bud. *I wouldn't do that now,* Steve said, much later; *I'd just
tell her I'm not firing it.* During a lecture in advanced ceramics

on the surface tension of holes, Steve showed us images
of British sculptor and photographer Andy Goldsworthy's

site-specific land art pieces: his autumn leaves
fanned into a solar eclipse around a black circle of soil;

his mound of pebbles piled to frame a hole; his woven
twig tapestry hung from a tree branch in the shape

of a spider web. Goldsworthy, Steve said, tries to look
through the surface appearance of things by introducing

a hole, a window that accentuates the mystery. After Steve's
two-year visiting professorship ended and he moved

with his wife from Virginia to Michigan,
all I saw were holes in the campus ceramics studio:

in the wheel-head Steve used for demos, the center
where his hands once hovered; in the enormous

gas kiln Hamada—which Steve taught me to load
and fire—each time I opened its steel door to find

an empty chamber; even in my own work
that resembled his so closely my classmate Julie

mocked my Shino-glazed coffee mugs and their squiggly
iron oxide brushwork—*Where's Steve?* she taunted,

picking up a mug. *Oh, wait. He's right here!* Even though
I saved plenty of my old pots, I always sip coffee

from one of Steve's mugs. For the past twenty years,
each day I fit my right thumb into the divot

his made when he pressed the top of the soft
handle into the body. He liked to say

our objects of domestic use have *a deep-rooted
common language,* that we create intimacy

with people through clay's tactile qualities. I left
that language for another, for the one

I'm using now. Although Julie was mean, she was right,
really, about those shapes—they belonged to Steve,

placeholders for a hand-shaped hole. Andy Goldsworthy
refers to *this void, this negative area* in his artwork's

surfaces as *a window into what lies below.* Long ago,
when Steve told me he'd deliberately chipped

Jen's "bud vase," for a minute I wondered
if that bong's cracked lip—too fractured

to press to a face—finally moved her to slip
into the belly's small hole the single stem of a rose.

Make It Blue

If you can't make it good,
make it big. If you can't make it big,
make it blue. You're thinking
of that old joke from art school,
the one that mocks the amateur-
potter-at-the-craft-fair trope
and the customers who hunt
for coffee mugs glazed
their favorite color: blue. You
repeated the mantra after
your teacher Steve said it, slung it
around the ceramics studio
to laughter. Years later, you can't
make it good or big. It's June.
The cases of the virus
are on another "uptick,"
so all you make now
comes out blue. You knew
back in art school it was the color
no self-respecting potter
would reach for and so you
glazed everything Shino instead—
that warm taupe flecked
with brick red and cream. Make it blue
was the punch line. You seem
to recall there wasn't a single
bucket of blue in the glaze room,
though in fact there must've
been one, untouchable, shoved
in a back corner. Did someone scrawl
on its lid: *This Will Match*
Your Grandma's Curtains?
Was it you? But you can't make it
good or big and there's an uptick.

There's a cop's knee pressed
on a man's neck. You'd glaze
all the date palms of deep June blue,
the whole Year of the Rat, the adjective
you wish you had no business
knowing: zoonotic. You'd choose
that pariah color you avoided
throughout art school although
it was secretly your favorite.
I'm making it now, Steve, you'd say,
in degrees of taboo—French blue,
navy, slate, or cornflower. Prussian,
powder, royal, sky, or spruce. You
can't make it good or big and so
you're dipping your wrists in,
then sinking them deeper. *Steve,*
you'd say, *this time I'm finally*
making it blue.

Elegy for Paul, Who Died without a Stomach

What kind of dude, at twenty-eight, makes butternut squash
soup on Friday night? You, Paul:

grad student, poet, former chef. You knew
to add Spanish onion, unsalted butter, thyme,

heavy cream, a bay leaf. You knew,
before baking, to drape each

halved squash in thin pancetta. I didn't know
a person could even *put*

cooked squash in a blender. I didn't break
up with my boyfriend then,

but I made him stay
home the night of your whiskey-

tasting party. Although whiskey
makes me mean, makes me

throw things, I came anyway,
sipped whatever

peat-and-vanilla burn
in a tumbler you poured. Forty, Paul,

is an unacceptable age to die
from stomach cancer, from

anything at all. After your death,
I read your food blog. Your last recipe:

lamb tenderloin with herb
spätzle and radishes. In the photo

of the finished dish, you'd spread
ten fillets in symmetrical rows: five

on each side so the mirrored cuts
formed a ribcage over plump

German dumplings. I once
wrote your red Chelsea boots

into a poem, imagined
a leather fetish. I brought the piece

to class, hoped you'd notice. I left out
your Roman nose, your laugh

that was actually just a stuttered
exhalation of Camel smoke, your grey

rescue tabbies named in nerdy
homage to the English Romantics.

What the fuck, Paul? Forty?
I know I apologized long ago

for that time at Rudyard's pub
when I was drunk: I said Lord

Byron was boring and you leaned
forward, shook the ice-melt in your glass's

watered-down bourbon. *What are you,*
an anti-intellectual? I slapped

your left cheek. Paul, I never told you
that after your whiskey party,

I returned to my apartment
to find my lover

had hidden all of the knives.
I say this now—inappropriately and far

too late—as a sort of compliment,
and because I'd rather picture

those steel blades tucked away
instead of your yellowed face

swollen from chemo-bloat
in late photographs, or that gourmet

squash soup you stopped making
after the gastrectomy. You once told me

you used a spoon to scoop all the soft-
baked flesh from the skin of the gourd.

Portrait of an Ex-lover as a Hillbilly Satyr

You once hiked Appalachia in the hooves
you'd packed on our camping trip to Cascades Falls,

near Blacksburg, Virginia. You'd sneaked
your favorite family heirloom with us

from a locked trunk in your dad's garage: those black,
cap-toe oxfords your great-grandfather

the moonshiner altered, in 1924, to disguise
his footprints from cops. He'd carved a pair

of cow's hooves from two white oak blocks, nailed
the platform stamps to his leather soles. For years

he walked the Blue Ridge Highlands
to his whiskey still in a remote meadow and left

only animal tracks. Your dad had never let you wear
the moonshiner-shoes when you'd begged as a kid,

yet during my first visit to your childhood house
in those mountains, I dared you. *Come on! We'll just*

borrow them. You grabbed the trunk's key
from your dad's bedside drawer while he watched

TV. Each night of our three-day camping trip, we'd play
the same game at dusk: we'd sip

from our flask, I'd slip into the tent and count
to fifty. You'd pick one of the mountain trails and set out

wearing your hooves, your red beard, your
red plaid, *like a hillbilly satyr,* you'd joke as you strapped

a soprano ukulele to your back. The trick
was to see if I could tell the faux bovine

prints in mud from the cloven shapes of the real
ungulates. You were easy to follow because

you always wound up at the sheet-mossed
bottom of the falls, your chin tipped toward

the top of the sixty-foot cliff, where the whitewater
began its wider feather and plunge. The last time

I found you, you didn't notice me, didn't hear me
creep up the creek-side path. I watched you wait

near a limestone crag shaggy with rock-cap ferns
for a full minute without speaking. Your warm

shoulders steamed where they shrugged
off the creek's cool mist, your right hoof

raised on a granite boulder. Something soft
in your face told me if I spoke then, you'd balk

and bellow. I knew your hooves—no longer oak—
had grown into your anklebones and marrow.

Mea Culpa: Final Offering to the One-Eyed Horse

I knew I wasn't supposed to approach
Kitzy from her blind side without
making a noise, without letting her

know I was there. I was ten
and often got stuck riding
the naughtiest strawberry roan

at the stables. Kitzy had only one eye
and liked to nip my right bicep
when I'd tighten her saddle's girth.

She'd "bloat" on purpose
as I buckled the cinch, then suck
her puffed belly back in

as she began to trot, which caused
the whole get-up to loosen and slide.
I'm not sure if Kitzy was born

one-eyed or if she'd caught moon
blindness as an adult or if a blackberry
bramble once tore her left cornea

during a canter at Angelica Run.
But I do know she was some
kind of hellion sent

to torment me. From the right side,
Kitzy's chestnut-and-white-pepper coat
made her look like a romantic

red beach pony and from the left,
her empty socket gaped with slivered
humps of slate-grey muscle and a fur

of blond dust, her third eyelid
dried into an iron curl—a kind of
conglomerate lash. Once I had

an impulse while alone with Kitzy
in her stall: to dart forward, silently,
and blow a sudden breath right into the hole

of her missing eye. Kitzy arched her neck,
bobbed her head, the skin over
her withers twitching. A spatter of grit

from the cavity slapped back
at my own face, sanded my eyes. I stroked
her muzzle, muttered, *Good girl,*

tried to justify my crime: I bet flies
flicker in and out of there
all the time. I'd like to leave

that moment behind, but I'd be lying
if I said I didn't sometimes
daydream my own underworld

whose iron sliding-gate rises
behind its red sentinel: Kitzy
waiting for me with her one

good eye. Only this time, I don't
blow into her empty socket. Instead,
I find in the center of a horse ring

adjacent to the gate a single hazel eye,
broad as a softball, and I run past
the other animals to scoop up Kitzy's

long-lost part. I approach with my offering,
drop the eye into her left socket and she blinks,
slowly nods. I know as I mount her,

without a saddle, that I've finally
paid for our passage, and the gate,
like a roan's third eyelid, slides open.

Dead Man's Lashes

Sometimes I blink and feel my papaw blink
from my face. He gave me

his wavy hair, his blond eyelashes
crooked as the state

of Mississippi. I didn't realize the curse
could be passed on: genetically

inward-growing eyelashes
that stab the corneas, lashes so bent

and mutinous they can ulcerate the eye,
scar the whites. During my eyelash-removal

treatments, called cryosurgeries, a doctor
freezes parts of my upper lids,

targets the follicles of the jagged lashes,
which drop off at the root. My papaw,

who lived in rural Greenwood,
had an optometrist neighbor who'd visit

every few weeks and insist on plucking
the old man's warped eyelashes for free

with a sterile tweezer. The last time my doctor
dripped Freon along my lids and the crooked

hairs fell, I blinked for a whole year
without a single bad stab or poke, until,

one by one, the dead man's lashes
began to push their way back up.

Autograph, Kansas City

for Paul Soldner

Followed the married man I puppy-loved
at twenty-one—my college pottery teacher,
Steve—to Kansas City

for a conference on ceramic art,
where my clay-friends and I slept
four to a hotel bed, when we slept

at all. Between Michele and Julie, I tried
to adjust to being not-naked
beneath the sheets. I flopped

in my courtesy underwear
and oversized t-shirt, thought of Steve's
wheel-throwing demos in class

when he'd point to and name each part
of a pot: *the lip, the neck, the belly, the foot.*
I'd tried not to notice the corresponding

spots on my body
quiver as he talked. So at the conference
when I walked into the convention hall and saw

posters of naked people all over a display table—
the nudes posed in humorous tableaux—
I had to stop for a look. The photographs

were outrageous ads for clay mixers placed
in a stack next to a white-bearded artist. I realized
the man signing posters with a fat

black marker was Paul Soldner, major figure
from the 1950s Clay Revolution who'd also
invented studio equipment and had his own line

of pottery wheels and clay mixers. He was famous,
too, for streaking the annual conference
dance, for throwing nipple-high floor pots

while shirtless, for raku firing in Aspen wearing only
a black Speedo. This was Soldner's Zen. So when
a tall vessel collapsed at the wheel, he'd carve up

the blob and reimagine it as a wall plaque
or pedestal piece made of folds, twists,
torn edges, and wings. And maybe he'd press

the side of a student's sneaker into the clay
for texture. During firing he welcomed spontaneous
shades that flashed across the glaze

when he dropped a red-hot piece into a raku pit,
which flamed. *Complete control,* Soldner said once,
is in conflict with the creative act. At the table, I picked

the poster I liked best from the stack: an ad
for one of Soldner's jacuzzi-sized clay mixers.
In the photograph, captioned *Still Streaking*

After All These Years, the buck-naked artist
reclines, grinning, in a baby carriage—one of those
three-wheeled jogging strollers. Two

hugely pregnant nude women push him
across a stage on which a professorial man
at a podium appears to be giving

a lecture on art, a slide of a ceramic sculpture
projected on a screen. As Soldner leans
back in the baby stroller, his posture

satirizes a classic odalisque: one arm raised
suggestively, hand cupped behind
his head. The bump of his potbelly echoes

the pregnant women's two
rounded torsos. I grinned and passed
the poster to the seated artist, watched him scrawl

his last name and the year: *Soldner '02*. Before he
gave me the signed ad, he glanced up,
then down, quickly pulled out of his pants

a cigarette lighter and flicked it, burned
a small hole in the paper, just below his signature,
as a kind of expressionist flourish.

He blew out the flame before
anyone else noticed. The burn-mark had a charred
halo around it, with an irregular quarter-sized

oval I could peep through. I moved
that poster to every apartment and house
thereafter, taped it to at least five different

living room walls. I finally lost track of the ad
when I was almost forty. By then Soldner
was dead ten years and I hadn't touched

clay in fifteen. I can't explain why I'm now
trying to find that old poster, which I probably
rubber-banded and forgot in some box. It's not

the nude bodies I'm looking for, or the artist's
autograph, or even the charred mark he left
in response to a young potter's

sly grin. I'd like to peer again
through that eye-sized hole and watch as I walk
out of the convention hall and into the Kansas

City night, where I stand alone, briefly,
beneath a streetlight, lift that burned paper
to my face for a sniff. I want to know if

that's the moment I first understood Soldner's
invitation—and that his call to fill that blank
would last the rest of my life.

four

Hans Christian Andersen Feared Being Buried Alive

I, too, Hans Christian,
once left a warning note. Your bedside

table's scribble read, *I only appear*
to be dead—an effort to ward off

the would-be pallbearers
who'd drop you

into your grassy plot in Nørrebro,
forgetting to check your nostrils

with a hand mirror for a fog
of breath. You dreaded

startling awake, six feet of Denmark
on your chest. At seventeen,

I stuck my own note
to the base of a blue

ceramic toothbrush holder:
Don't forget to brush

in small, soft circles. As a child,
I'd chipped my right front tooth

and incisor on a pool's
concrete edge and had grown

phobic about further
eroding my smile. I worried

that if I came home at midnight
still tripping from a five-strip

of blotter acid, I might brush
maniacally and scrape

off chunks of gum,
my loosened teeth dropping

to the porcelain sink bowl,
like bloody dominoes. I might

wake up the next day
with a corpse-face. It's important,

Hans Christian, to have a system,
a reminder: a few words written

to catch the eye and hold
back the hand that would bury us.

Bathtub Elegy

When my neighbor Kay's boyfriend OD'd in their clawfoot,
she and her three brothers dragged the cast iron

bulk to the front yard of her row house in Richmond,
painted the enamel lavender. *I can't bathe*

in that thing again, Kay said when I brought
rhubarb cobbler to her door. She'd transformed

the tub into a planter for a single crop:
a fattening spread of spearmint. *He's dead,*

Kay said, *so I'm drinking nothing*
but mojitos the rest of the summer. The cocktail

was Dave's favorite. Halfway through June I knew
I had to stop sitting on my front stoop at night

since the bathtub sat just on the other side
of our shared iron fence. During the day,

the sun would bake the spearmint into a fragrance
so sweet and alive I was sure if I lingered

at night I'd see the clawfoot begin to crabwalk
across the grass, trailing its wake of mint

and flaked paint as if scattering some last
crumbs for Dave to follow.

I Ship My Parents the Granulated Urine of Carnivores

Not for luck, like a rabbit's white foot,
and not as a sick joke about telling the year

2020 to piss off. I'd like to help my folks
scare away that one deranged grey squirrel

that lives in their backyard and compulsively
gnaws long swaths of their yellow

fiber-cement siding as if trying to erode
the whole damn house. I thought of those

applewood chew sticks I used to drop
on the pine mulch of my hamster Cuddles'

aquarium as a treat. They were supposed to
reduce boredom and help him file

his incisors so the teeth wouldn't grow
through the roof of his palate, stab

his brain. He'd always gnaw the fragrant sticks
down to the last splinter. I worry now

about my dad's spiked blood
pressure each time he hears the squirrel's

manic crunch and grabs his BB gun.
He runs, red-faced, into the yard to chase

the rodent back to its stand of crepe myrtles
and sugar maples. I've read about organic

modes of pest control, like the giant
spice-shakers of dried urine flakes

from bobcats, foxes, and coyotes. You sprinkle
the pee around borders of zucchini patches

or beds of pink impatiens you don't want
eaten or dug up. The deer and rodents trust

their noses, believe death edges close. I chose
from the carnivores the fiercest

specimen I could find: wolf. Next month
marks a year since I've seen my parents

because of the threat of the virus. I don't like them
going out. I don't like that goddamn

lunatic squirrel gnawing their house as if
appointed by the Year of the Rat

as mascot of total destruction. I don't need
help in that department, buddy. I need

a vaccine, Christmas outside
of a laptop screen. Until then I'll settle

for a circle of wolves, a scent that says:
Cross this threshold's ammonia and I'll go for your throat.

My Dulcimer Teacher Joellen Works as a Psychotherapist

which means a creek constantly talks
from a table in the waiting room Joellen shares
with another therapist. The waters slosh

and eddy from one of those white noise
machines with settings like *Ocean,*
Thunder, Rain, Summer Night, and *Brook.*

The two shrinks always flood
their office suite above a Persian café
in Westwood with *Brook.* They submerge

and whitewater patients' voices
for privacy, so nosy, amateur
Appalachian dulcimer players won't spy

on the confessions. I confess: A river
once spoke over me. This was back
in Virginia, in the tannic

shallows of a brown river named
for an English king—James. That mix
of coal ash and factory runoff always made

wading into a dare. This is where,
summer nights, my best friend Alicia and I
sat up to our hips in the current

as we clutched our beer bottles
and sliced limes, repeated the same
toast in honor of the polluted river:

Don't get it in your holes! I only remember
the joke now in overdub. The rapids'
loud static hides my old

self from myself. What were we
talking about, anyway, at dusk, in Richmond,
at twenty-three? Was it the story

in which I leap from a pin oak's rope-swing
into deep water, scrape my big toe
on the plywood jumping-platform, suffer

the nickname Swamp Foot
for the rest of the year? Here, in L.A.,
our creek beds lie parched, mute,

yet in the waiting room the brook
keeps up its ciphering. I haven't told
Joellen I've secretly dragged

that water for a body. I never know
if there's an actual patient sitting
behind the second door, waist-deep

in her own story, about to open
her mouth to speak even
as the river rushes in to fill it.

Retro Acoustics with Too Much Nitrogen
in the Mix (Listening to My Ex's New Album,
Music to Help Plants Grow)

Here it is: his voice summoned
by a click, a white bud
stuck in each ear. At first, I laughed

at one song's title, "Gimmie Back
My Compost Heap," recalling
how furious Patrick had gotten

when our landlord's gardener
mowed our row house's backyard
and mistook the compost heap

for a garbage mound—that mountain
of scraps and soil lumped along
one side of the yellow-pine fence. The problem:

Patrick had skipped the step
in which you're supposed to chop up
food waste before adding it

to the pile. He'd toss in whole
corncobs, banana peels, garlic husks,
eggshells, watermelon rinds.

I didn't mind the stink too much
since we had a concrete slab instead
of a screened porch and so rarely

risked the backyard's hammock
and its humid static of mosquitoes.
Although that compost heap was more

nitrogen than carbon, more
slowly decomposing proteins
than branches and leaves, I liked

how Patrick nourished the dark mound
as he would a living creature, how he
proudly addressed its potential

to become nutrient-rich humus. *Soon
we'll have a pile of black gold,* he'd say,
as he patted the heap and planned

the ways he'd transform our patch
of ryegrass with its lone crepe myrtle
into a vegetable garden flanked

by sunflowers. But I could understand
why someone would mistake
his grungy mishmash of foodstuffs

rotting in the August heat
for a miniature landfill. We'd stayed
at the river all afternoon, returned

to find a freshly mown lawn
and a clean-swept rectangle of soil
where the ziggurat of ripe table scraps

had moldered. Patrick raged,
kept sputtering, *They stole my compost heap!*
When confronted, our landlord forbade us

from starting another fly-buzzed mass.
Since Patrick was a jazz and bluegrass
musician from the mountains of southwest

Virginia, I figured he'd improvised
with soil the way he'd layered the woo-woo
of a musical saw with acoustic

guitar chords or mournful whistles
in a recorded track, that he
didn't care to follow the rules

of a balanced compost heap
whose ideal ratio—one-third green
materials and two-thirds brown—

meant to prevent a dense and foul-
smelling anaerobic disaster: a black
garbage peak. *Gimmie back*

my compost heap, goes the song,
Gimmie back my dirt.
Gimmie back my Mother Earth

or else you're gonna get hurt. I heard
a little of Kurt Cobain's raw
Americana in the vocal track—

Nirvana's haunting cover of "In the Pines,"
combined with the absurdist
verve of Captain Beefheart. I'd startled

at the edge of menace in the verse's
last line, but the song
then enlarges from personal

grudge to a broader lament
for the destruction of the Blue Ridge
due to mountaintop removal mining—

that coal industry practice he'd watched
grind down Appalachia.
On our first long hike together

outside of Blacksburg, his hometown,
I noticed Patrick's habit of patting
and shaking the green tops of saplings

along the trail: his invented superstition
meant to help young trees grow. I know
he must've loved that stinking

compost heap anarchic with old
garlic and brown banana peels
the way he loved jamming

on his upright bass during a bluegrass
show with his string band, his eyes
closed, his auburn beard bobbing.

He probably didn't think to read
through the rules of proper composting
because he knew nature

had always been an improviser.
I never minded that rotten imbalance
of nitrogen darkening one half

of our yard. Years later, on hikes
I can't stop reaching out
to shake every sapling I pass.

Bodywork

One year married, we walked among humid bones
of the Paris Catacombs. To reach the tunnels
and subterranean galleries, David and I
had to climb five stories down, in a winding line
of other tourists. Only a small group of us
could descend the stairs at once,
so we wouldn't breathe up too much oxygen
that deep underground. There, my neck's

nape turned clammy, my wrist-hair
slick in a nylon camera-strap. We moved
through the old limestone quarries packed
with ancient skeletons—the bones dug up
from overflowing cemeteries in Paris
and dumped in the abandoned tunnels,
later arranged into decorative walls of alternating
skulls and tibiae. Workers

had emptied the stinking graveyards in the late
eighteenth century, after the reek of human remains
strained sales even at the perfume shops
and the spring rains bloated the soil,
scenting the market at Les Halles
with corpses. The workers

had to move the bodies into the ossuary
at night, so as not to shock the public
or infuriate the Church. I couldn't believe

tourists actually took photographs of themselves
with the skeletons, grinning and posing
in front of human bones
as if for a family portrait. *Look
at those assholes,* I hissed

to David, as another American couple
smiled with someone's fractured cranium
framed between their faces.

::

It used to bother me when lovers
got a "couple's massage" on a mat
near mine at Raven Spa, only a few
floor-length curtains tugged between us.
I'd go there biweekly to manage
my back pain with a ninety-minute
traditional Thai from Zy, who I called
"my healer" to friends, only
half-jokingly. It drove me crazy:

that pillow-talk interrupting the rush
of water from the terracotta fountain's
three spouted lion-heads. Mostly, the couples
murmured *Love you* or *baby* to each other
before or after their massage
as I breathed into the pressure
of a digging elbow. The overlapping
curtains sometimes left a gap
and I accidently glimpsed a hand,
a foot, a kiss. Although I'm far
from Buddhist, I liked to lose
myself in the quiet, the relief
when a fibrous knot would finally release,
and the warm brown tea, afterward,
in a glass tumbler beside a teak plate
of dates and sliced apple.

During my last visit before
the virus shuttered the spa,
I listened as two lovers finished
their couple's massage and then began
a low-grade fight. One woman asked
the other in a note of paranoid
spite: *What were you thinking about
the whole time?*

::

A visit to the Paris Catacombs should,
according to the official website,
prompt *visitors toward introspection
and a meditation on death.* When David and I
reached the algaed Fountain of Lethe

I almost tossed in a penny, but didn't want to
forget my life. I took
only a few photographs, neither of us
in them: just a close-up of one wall—the tibiae
stacked lengthwise, as if their outward-facing knobs
forever waited for sockets—and another
of the fountain, squat as a medieval
well. In 1813, mining engineer
Héricart de Thury dropped four goldfish

into the Fountain of Lethe as an experiment,
to see if they'd survive down in the catacombs
without any light. The fish lived,
but they could no longer reproduce
and completely lost their sight. After our tour,
David and I sat in a café without speaking
of the dead, squinted in mid-afternoon sun

that seemed to heat our skin
into forgetting. As we'd ascended the steps
back into the world of traffic and flesh
all we'd said was: *I'm starving* and *How bright.*

My Ugly

I picked Dockweiler Beach, the ugliest one
within a fifteen-minute drive, so David and I could touch

our bare feet to hot sand for the first time
since the virus hit Los Angeles. We knew tourists

would swarm the fancy beaches farther north,
even in the middle of an outbreak, so we stayed away

from Venice, Santa Monica, and Malibu—destination
spots with restaurants and boardwalks, rooftop

cocktails and boutique hotels, couples posed for mauve
sunsets on the piers. David and I hoped to disappear

into a lesser-known shoreline, forget about contagion
and his asthma for an hour as we sat

in canvas folding chairs and stared at the cold
Pacific rolling in. I found the perfect isolated beach

between two industrial processing plants, one water,
one power: Dockweiler Beach's three-mile stretch

that runs next to the main take-off strip of LAX.
Each time a jet blared overhead, clusters

of gulls and Caspian terns barely glanced up
from the sand, balanced on one leg and completely

immune to the engine's noise. They sat in loose groups,
facing the waves with the poise of transcendental

meditators among crumbles of greased
styrofoam and shards of metal. We plopped

our chairs down, leaving at least fifty feet
on both sides from other locals and arranged

ourselves within a horseshoe formation
of shorebirds: the poop-threat, we hoped, would keep

people away. Between Dockweiler Beach and the airport
lies the eroded ghost town of Surfridge:

that 1920s colony of seaside mansions
razed in the late sixties and early seventies

because of expanding jet traffic, which rattled
the houses' windowpanes, erased whole

conversations. The airport drove away homeowners
with forced condemnations and mandatory buyouts.

All that's left of the once-stately neighborhood
is its ocean view, with a few cracked

and weed-split streets, knee-high ryegrass,
oxtongue, and bull thistle. And among

the scattered queen palms: some remaining
lampposts with Doric columns of fluted iron

and empty globes of opaque glass. The ghost
town's now a chain-linked nature preserve

for the endangered El Segundo blue butterfly.
I'd expected extreme degrees of ugly at the beach,

but each time the low path of a military helicopter
hugged the coastline, the Caspian terns

alighted and wheeled in a helix of tiny
porcelain darts as the black choppers passed.

And I admired the tragedy performed
behind us, whose exclusive cast comprised

a troupe of blue butterflies that flitted
through the not-even-ruins, the total absence

of a six-thousand-foot Spanish-Moroccan
mansion that locals once called "the Castle,"

which LAX bought for eighty-six grand and bulldozed
flat. As we watched the Caspian terns regroup

and resume their meditation in the sand, I told David
about my grandmother's favorite piece

of costume jewelry: the necklace she bought
in 1960s Jackson, Mississippi, picked

from a display case of love beads, mood rings,
and peace-sign pins. It was a clay pendant

glazed a matte grey and shaped like a stylized
oblong skull or shrunken head with cheeks

gaunt as a mummy's. Its buglike close-set
eye sockets, crosshatched oval nose, and mouthless chin

radiated a goofy primitivist humor. My granny
strung the pendant on a black leather cord

and called the whimsical death's-head necklace
her "ugly." She wore the ugly when she dressed up,

even to church. I like to think of her ugly
as a talisman, a way to ward off evil the way,

years later, I chose a grimy industrial beach
in L.A. for protection. Without the virus

I never would've known about the ghost town
only fifteen minutes from my house and I've lived

in this city ten years. I never would've known
the El Segundo blue butterfly is slowly resurrecting

its species in the jet-shaken weeds below iron
lampposts someone decided to leave there to light

no one's path. As we packed up our canvas chairs,
I thought if I could stare over my shoulder

at a globe long enough at dusk, one would flare
as a sign from the ghosts in their razed town,

who promise to wait on the cusp of the ugliest beach
for as long as we need them and keep watch.

For the Actor Luke Perry, Who Chose to Be Buried in a Biodegradable Funeral Suit Infused with Mushroom Mycelia

Luke, I've been thinking of your green
burial lately, the taupe shapes your afterlife
must take as it grows in soft lobes
up sassafras, black walnut, and beech trees

in Vanleer, Tennessee. Your family
kept your gravesite's location private,
so some punk won't pilgrimage there, hoping
to pluck the clusters of shiitake or white button

you've become, the enoki or reishi.
Luke, you know the bodies of Italian saints
displayed in Snow White coffins of glass
for tourists to gawk at in Rome? I never saw

God in the magic of an incorruptible corpse
which of course has always been
a performance: the prune-textured flesh
of St. Paula Frassinetti regularly bathed

in carbolic acid for the last century.
Roman Catholics used to believe
holiness could keep a saint's body
from decomposing. But, Luke,

I like your attitude. It's less *Can't take it
with you,* more *Please receive
this gift, this body of holy compost.* Alms
for the wounded planet. Luke,

I should tell you two things.
The first is: A year or so before
your fatal stroke and during an earnest
craze I'll call "my mushroom phase"

I bought myself an Infinity
Burial Suit, courtesy of my university
research account—same 'shroom-infused
pajamalike model you later got

in biodegradable black cotton. Like other
expensive formal outfits I've worn
only once, it hangs
among cocktail dresses in my home

office's closet. The second
thing is: As a child I owned your effigy,
your image cast in plastic for Mattel's
1991 celebrity-Barbie that portrays

your character on *Beverly Hills, 90210,* the sexy
rebel Dylan McKay. Confession: I once
dressed and undressed you, Luke, and I saw
what I knew, even at ten, wasn't

every body part, just a tan band
between your hairless thighs smooth
and neutral as a roll of packing tape. By now,
Luke, I've seen more detailed rolls

of packing tape than *that,* and all your parts
are now part of the Big Mystery,
freer than St. Paula still stuck in her
carbolic myth. I've learned some mushrooms

enrich the topsoil through their role
as decomposers—they help break down
rotten logs and dead animals. The fungi
degrade carbon-based toxins, too,

including the petroleum products
and industrial chemicals we absorb
through our skin, carry in our bloodstreams
throughout our lives. One of my

favorite fairy tale illustrations
is a lithograph by Russian artist
Ivan Bilibin—his portrait of Baba Yaga,
the Slavic witch, who hovers

in her airborne spice mortar above
a crop of red-capped toadstools
in a mossed wood. The framed print
hangs near my kitchen's stainless

steel gas range, that mix of the old
world and the new. Now,
when I stand at the stovetop, stirring
a sauté, I glance at the enchanted

mushroom-swarmed forest, Luke,
and think of you. I don't only
recall your heartthrob Barbie doll, all
cragged and broody profile and miniature

red corduroy zip-jacket. I think
of your late-in-life incarnation
as ecological ambassador
to the underworld who has already,

and unlike the preserved Roman
saints behind glass, returned without
a shinbone or a wisdom tooth intact
but as risen flesh, shape-shifting, everlasting.

Cherry Angiomas

Those pinpoint red
flecks on my belly, my thighs,

my forearms' sides and white
undermeat. They're called

cherry angiomas—skin-growths
comprised of overzealous

blood vessels, clusters
of capillaries like tiny,

bright moles. Also known as—
to my horror and to spite

all vanity—senile angiomas,
since they stipple the flesh

of people over thirty
years old. It's when I began

to notice my belly's red marks
I started to seek out

cherries everywhere. I'd add three
to my Manhattan's spicy rye,

a crop to the cobblers
I baked, uncharacteristically,

all April and May of the virus,
dry-mixing the sugar

and flour, a single
fruit to the hour

it takes me to fall asleep,
repeating the name of my favorite

street in Richmond:
South Cherry. I don't know

much about skin,
but I know how to go on

living in it. I like the flaw's
first and kinder name. I like

the language that says I'm
blood-red fruit, blooming.

CPSIA information can be obtained
at www.ICGtesting.com
Printed in the USA
LVHW032035220222
711687LV00004B/437